THIS BOOK BELONGS TO:

_____

_____

HAND ME DOWN

_____

Written by Amy Morrison. With consulting from Julia Moss.

ISBN: 979-8-9867049-1-3
LCCN: 2022918218

This book was printed in China in November 2022.

First edition
6 5 4 3 2

For questions regarding permissions, sales, or discounts,
email us at hello@littlefeminist.com.

LITTLE FACES
BIG FEELINGS

WHAT EMOTIONS LOOK LIKE

By Amy Morrison

little feminist press

Nico seems happy. Would you agree?
Everyone here feels very carefree.

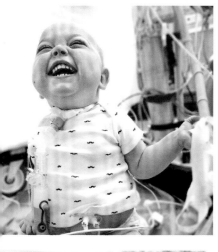

Jayla looks sad. What could we say?
"How can I help?" might be useful today.

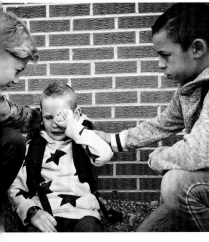

Mad or frustrated? Can you tell?
Big emotions can make us yell.

Jordan's surprise is easy to see.
What do you think the best surprise would be?

Feeling scared is okay. No feeling is wrong.
Emotions give clues about what's going on.

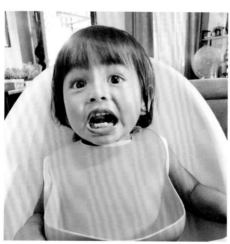

Being brave doesn't mean that you're not afraid.
Sometimes things feel scary but we try anyway.

Bored sometimes feels like nothing to do.
When someone looks bored we might try something new

Silly is jumping and twirling and fun.
Who do you think looks silly? Does everyone?

Stevie seems tired after a long day at play.
It's time for some sleep. What did you feel today?

A NOTE FOR GROWNUPS

The media surrounding us has a tendency to stereotype races, genders, and abilities (to name a few). For example, we often see people with disabilities portrayed as brave but they can feel happy too. On our screens and in our books, we often see people of color who are mad or frustrated, but they can be silly too! Let's stop stereotypes in their tracks — point out stereotypes when you see them and discuss them with your littles.

ABOUT LITTLE FEMINIST

LittleFeminist.com is a children's book club subscription and publishing house. Our team curates the best diverse books, creates accompanying discussion questions and activities, and delivers to families around the world. We publish books to fill the gaps we find in children's literature.

Photo Acknowledgements: Amanda Kahl Smith; Amy Park; Annemarie Govardhan; Ashley Renee Jefferson; Cheryl Lala; Courtney Fujikawa; Crystal Costante; Emily Meagher; @itsjazzme03 (Philippines); Kati Douglas; Keshnee Naidoo; Lisa Rodriguez; Natalie Gochez; Nayeli Bernal; Scot Goodman; Susannah Kay. Additional photos from Shutterstock and Stocksy.

FAMILY DISCUSSION QUESTIONS

BABIES & TODDLERS

Use the mirror at the back of this book to practice happy, sad, mad, bored, tired, and surprised faces with your little. You can make this a guessing game too.

Use the feelings wheel at the back of the book to practice labeling emotions. You can make this a game too. For example, while playing peek-a-boo you might say "Uh oh, where's Dada? Here I am! Are you surprised? Are you happy you found me?"

2 - 4 YEAR OLDS

What is something that happened today that maybe made you feel _____?

Crank up the music and feel how your bodies and emotions change. Start with upbeat tunes, then dial back the tempo with relaxing music. Talk about how each song makes you feel.

4 - 6 YEAR OLDS

If you are feeling sad, mad/frustrated, scared, or bored what helps you? When I get mad, I take deep breaths (use your own example). What do you like to do?

Ask your little(s) what their emotions look and feel like. This helps us verbalize and process our feelings. For example: What does mad look like to you? What color would silly be? What do you feel in your body when you are bored?

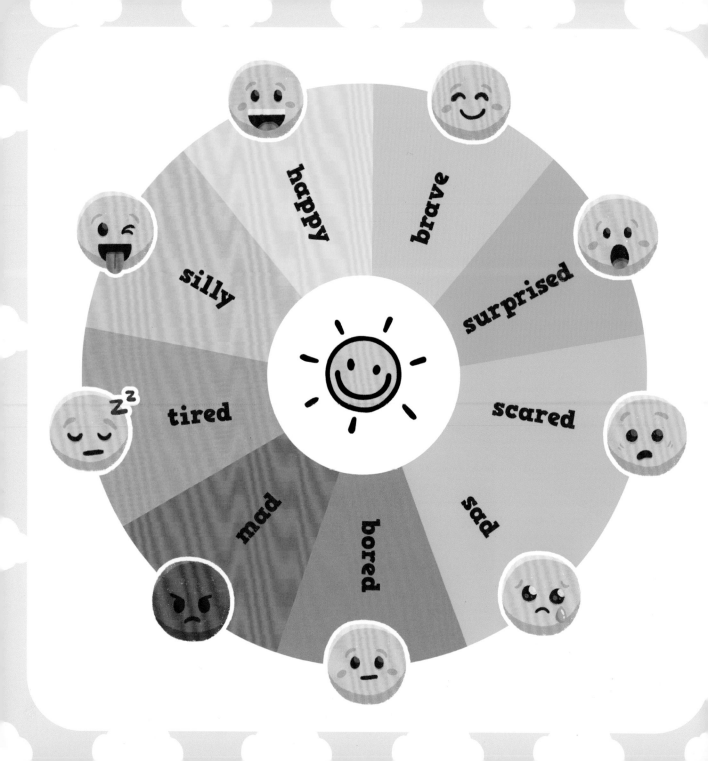